BALTIMORE & OHIO HERITAGE 1945-1955

BY JOHN KRAUSE AND ED CRIST

PHOTOGRAPHY BY ROBERT F. COLLINS, AND JOHN KRAUSE

Second Printing 1986

ISBN No. 911868-52-6

FREDON-SPRINGDALE ROAD FREDON TOWNSHIP
P O BOX 700, NEWTON N J 07860

JOHN KRAUSE

INTRODUCTION

The Baltimore and Ohio was a pioneer in the use of diesel-electric locomotives as road power on passenger trains. Yet steam locomotives lasted well into the 1950's, longer than on most American Class One railroads. The transition era when the railroads were turning more and more to the diesel was by far the most interesting time for the railroad photographer, for once the fires on the last steam locomotives had died it would never again be possible to see the mixing of the two eras.

When roads such as the Erie and the Lackawanna had turned the steamers out to pasture in the early 1950s, the photographers turned to the B&O for the final years of steam power in action. By the time the final steam locomotive had been pulled from service, hundreds of pictures had been taken of the transition era by many of the outstanding photographers in the railroad field. We have made a selection of photographs from several of the cameramen from hundreds of excellent negatives selected for use. These selected photographs offer a look back on the Baltimore and Ohio when steam and diesel worked hand in hand on the oldest railroad in the United States.

Pioneer diesels, speeding President Class Pacifics, pounding freight locomotives and the smaller branch line locomotives, they are all here. The Central Railroad of New Jersey played host to the crack passenger terminal. While Jersey City was a far cry from Pennsylvania station and Grand Central Terminal in New York, it was, none the less, a most interesting place to encounter the B&O. Here one could find the streamlined diesels ready to haul the Diplomat standing side by side with old camelback steamers of the Jersey Central, a sight surely not possible at the midtown terminals of the Pennsylvania and the New York Central. Here we look back in time, to the era when steam and diesel power were part of the Baltimore and Ohio Heritage.

John Krause and Ed Crist

William Mason ROBERT F. COLLINS

ROBERT F. COLLINS

Another President-class Pacific, the 5317, pauses for her portrait at Jersey City. The P-7 class 4-6-2's were delivered in the B&O's centenary year of 1927 by the Baldwin Works of Philadelphia. To celebrate its hundredth birthday the B&O had staged a million-dollar-party at a specially constructed grandstand at Halethorpe, Md. A mile of track circled the grounds and old and new locomotives and cars from both the B&O and other railroads passed in review before more than 12,000 spectators in the grandstands. The grand finale of each show consisted of the 5300, the *President Washington,* pulling six new cars of the *Capitol Limited* to a perfect stop in front of the stands. The engines were numbered from 5300 to 5319, twenty locomotives in all named for the first twenty-one presidents; the Adams' had to settle for one engine for both of them. Resplendent in olive green and gold striping, the Pacifics handled all of the B&O's name trains. In the late 1930's, the B&O re-equipped the Royal Blue train with streamlined equipment painted in a blue-and-gray scheme, the colors being chosen to represent both sides of the Mason-Dixon line. In 1941, new president Roy White ordered the engines to be painted blue to match the equipment and alas, he also ordered the names to be removed. The next major change came in 1944 and 1945 when some of the Presidents were completely rebuilt with one-piece cast steel engine beds. The engine bed, more commonly known as the frame, was traditionally made up of individual pieces secured by rivets and special tapered bolts, which proved to be a constant source of maintainance problems. In the late 1920's, casting technology had improved to the point where the entire bed could be cast as a single unit. Over the years, many older engines were rebuilt with the one-piece beds, which in many cases also included the cylinders. Other changes included roller bearings on some engines, a lowered headlight, and a repositioning of the air pumps to the pilot deck where they were safely tucked away behind a shield adorned with the B&O's capitol emblem. The 5317 shown above, once named the *President Hayes,* was part of a 1949-50 continuation of the rebuilding program that saw the reconditioned engines roll out of the shops with new and much larger tenders. The photo above dates to the spring of 1949 and 5317 is fresh from her facelifting only to see nine more years of active service.

ROBERT F. COLLINS

JOHN KRAUSE

TOP LEFT: Another portrait at the Jersey City engine terminal of the Jersey Central. The 57 and 57X must have looked strange indeed rubbing shoulders with the CNJ's aging fleet of Camelbacks. Back when an A and a B unit were considered to be one locomotive, B&O used the suffix "X" to denote the B unit, a practice finally discontinued in 1956 when a general renumbering of all locomotives, steam and diesel, took place. The 57 was an E-6 model passenger locomotive produced by the Electro-Motive Division of General Motors Corporation and part of a 1940 order by the B&O for eight sets (2nd 52, 57-63). The E-6 was EMD's first real production model passenger locomotive. The models before it were all one-shot deals built for individual railroads as the fledgling EMD worked the bugs out of its new line. Introduced in the fall of 1939, it was produced until the fall of 1942 when the War Production Board ordered the building of passenger locomotives to cease for the duration. BOTTOM LEFT: The same engines barking along through Bound Brook, N.J. on the CNJ. Bound Brook was the junction of the Reading line from Philadelphia with the CNJ main line to Jersey City and a Reading gas-electric car is just vaguely discernible in the distance. The tracks to the left are the parallel Lehigh Valley mains. The whole New York operation of the B&O had a rather long and interesting history. A through route was first established from Jersey City to Washington in the midst of the Civil War. However, the constant skirmishing with the Pennsylvania Railroad finally forced the B&O to lay its own rails to Philadelphia in 1886

and set up a through route with the Reading and Jersey Central. For many years afterwards, the B&O turned over its trains to a Reading locomotive at Park Junction in Philadelphia to forward the train to Bound Brook, where it would continue to Jersey City on the CNJ. The route was quite logical because the B&O owned a substantial interest in the Reading, which in turn owned the controlling interest in the Jersey Central. In the Centenary Year, 1927, the B&O decided to handle it all themselves and acquired trackage rights into Jersey City. This only lasted a few years after the B&O found that having trackage rights in New Jersey also meant paying Jersey taxes, the highest in the nation. They then decided to let their locomotives go on through with Reading and CNJ crews, the practice that remained in effect until the end of New York service in the late 1950's. The B&O's own Philadelphia Division and the Reading-CNJ line were the only place on the system where engines could scoop water "on the fly". A long trough was placed between the rails and filled with water. The tenders on the President engines were equipped with a scoop which could be dropped in the trough. At 50 or 60 mph, the incredible momentum of the train allowed the scoop to easily pick up 10,000 gallons or more of water in less than a minute. RIGHT: The 5305, once the *President Jackson,* is seen again laying down a cloud of smoke approaching Bound Brook. In the late 1940's, it was still common to see steam and diesel working together, a coexistence that would be all too brief.

JOHN KRAUSE

JOHN KRAUSE

ABOVE: It's another President-class Pacific rolling through the open countryside. But now it's Maryland we're in, birthplace of the B&O—the railroad had been conceived by a group of Baltimore businessman who could see that their continued prosperity would depend on a link to the great interior of the country. The infant B&O got not only a charter from the Maryland legislature, but a perpetual waiver of taxes. The former *President Van Buren,* no. 5306, was taken into the shop in 1942 and outfitted with a type R feedwater heater. This was one of the last of Col. George Emerson's long string of appliances that he designed over a 22-year tenure as B&O's motive power chief. The idea was to use the heat still remaining in the exhaust to warm up the boiler feedwater before finally exhausting the gases out the smokestack. It apparently didn't work well, for the 5306 as seen above in 1952 is plainly equipped with an Elesco heater that employs the exhaust steam from the cyclinders to do the heating rather than the more corrosive and destructive gases from the firebox. It's hard to come up with another road that did as much rebuilding and experimenting with its locomotive fleet as the B&O did under Emerson's term.

ROBERT F. COLLINS

ABOVE: Pacific no. 5000 pulling through a high-speed crossover at Orleans Road, West Virginia with a 14-car express train. The Potomac River, forming the boundary between Maryland and West Virginia, swings so far to the north that the B&O line from Baltimore to Cumberland had to cross the Potomac twice and pass through 20-some miles of West Virginia territory on its westward course. The 5000 was the first of the P-1c class engines, one of the B&O's more interesting rebuilds. The B&O had begun buying Pacifics in 1906 and continued to purchase them right through World War I. But the prosperity and heavy traffic of the 1920's necessitated even more passenger engines. The freight business was equally busy and between 1918 and 1923 the B&O had purchased 235 brand-new 2-8-2 Mikado freight engines. This left a number of older classes of "Mikes" that were not needed for freight work but that weren't ready for the boneyard either. Col. Emerson decided he could get new 4-6-2's at a bargain price by using the boilers of the old Mikados and mounting them on new running gear. The old boilers had good steaming capacity and coupled with the new wheel arrangement, they made an excellent heavy-duty passenger engine. In the early 1940's, some of the engines were given larger tenders and the class as a whole survived right through to the final days of steam. Also of note in this photo are the position-light signals mounted on the signal bridge itself. A vestige of the one-time Pennsylvania Railroad dominance of the B&O, the signals had an interesting double-barrelled indication. They displayed not only the traditional red-yellow-green aspect, but the position of the lights mimicked the traditional semaphore positions of horizontal-diagonal-vertical. Neither a burned out bulb nor a bad case of color blindness could result in a misreading of the indication. The first two cars behind the 5000 also have an interesting ancestry. Faced with huge passenger loads during World War II, the railroads found themselves with no equipment left to handle the equally large troop-train movements. The government came up with a design for troop sleepers and diners that weren't much more than a glorified boxcar, but they served the purpose. Of course, once the war was over the cars were of little use for any other service. However, they were already equipped with steam and signal lines and high-speed trucks for passenger service, so it was a relatively simple job to outfit them for express service. The four-tracking of the stretch of B&O main line from Cherry Run, West Virginia to Cumberland, Md. was one of the earliest accomplishments of the administration of Daniel Willard, who was to guide the fortunes of the B&O from 1910 to 1941.

JOHN KRAUSE

Cumberland, where the four tracks diverged into the two principal routes: the main through Grafton to Cincinnati and on to St. Louis and the main through Pittsburgh, Wheeling, and on to Chicago. Cumberland was a train-watcher's delight: mainline passenger trains, locals, hotshot freights, coal drags, pushers, and engines fresh from the giant locomotive shops of the city. ABOVE: We're standing at Cumberland station in 1948 to watch the parade. An E-6 diesel heading a through train is having her fuel tanks filled up for the forthcoming assault on Sand Patch grade. Down the other end of the platform, we find steam still in charge of a Baltimore local. The impressive brick station and hotel complex, for so many years a landmark in Cumberland, is now sadly just a memory. RIGHT: One of the B&O's monstrous EM-1's awaits clearance to pull through Cumberland on its way east. The EM-1's, nos. 7600-7629, were built by Baldwin in 1944 and 1945 and were one of the small number of 2-8-8-4's built. The 7607 has just come in from Grafton with a through freight from the St. Louis gateway. The line to Cincinnati and St. Louis and the branches of the West Virginia coal country deserve a volume of their own.

JOHN KRAUSE

JOHN KRAUSE

Stephen Grover Cleveland holds a unique spot in the list of American presidents. Elected as the 22nd president, he was beaten out by Benjamin Harrison, but after four years came back and beat Harrison to become the 24th president, the only man to ever serve two nonconsecutive terms of office. So it seems fitting that his name should adorn the cab sides of the last and most unusual of the President-class Pacifics. You will remember that the B&O had bought twenty new 4-6-2's in its centenary year of 1927; but a 21st locomotive would join the group a year later. In 1928, the historic Mt. Clare shops at Baltimore turned out the 5320, the *President Cleveland.* Col. Emerson had taken the boiler of Mikado 4201 and applied one of his famous water-tube fireboxes to it. The running gear underneath it was just as esoteric with its Caprotti valve gear. The Caprotti gear was imported from Italy and tried on a number of American roads without much success; in the case of the 5320, it lasted only a year before being replaced with the Walschaert's gear, which was curiously enough the invention of a Belgian. But the water-tube firebox stayed on the locomotive until 1945, one of the Colonel's more successful experiments. As the name implies, a water-tube firebox allows the heat to bear against water-filled tubes. In a conventional locomotive boiler, the hot gases passed through tubes surrounded by water. The water-tube firebox was not Col. Emerson's invention by any means: it had been used successfully for many years on marine and stationary boilers and the Colonel was convinced that it could be applied to locomotives. However, he failed to reckon with the widely varying output required of a locomotive boiler and his water-tube engines ran the gamut from successful to total disasters. In all, he designed and built a prophetic thirteen engines between 1927 and 1937. George H. Emerson was probably one of the most unusual and colorful men in American railroading. He was always referred to as "Col. Emerson", but the title was not of the bogus Kentucky variety; he had earned the rank serving with the Transportation Corps of the A.E.F. in Siberia, supervising the rebuilding of the Trans-Siberian Railway. The A.E.F. was working with the White Russian army in their aborted campaign of 1920 to recover their country from the Bolsheviks. Emerson had previously made quite a name for himself on the Hill lines in the West before going to Russia. Reportedly it was Samuel Vauclain, the grand old man of the Baldwin Locomotive Works, who told Daniel Willard to hire Col. Emerson, even going so far as to cable Emerson to return to the United States immediately. In any event, "Uncle Dan" was a veteran of Jim Hill's railroads himself and surely must have known of Emerson's reputation. The two men worked together for more than twenty years, each one holding his respective office longer than any other official in the B&O's entire 150-year history.

In 1937, the B&O retained the famous industrial designer Otto Kuhler to streamline the *Royal Blue.* To pull the streamlined heavyweight equipment, Mr. Kuhler took the 5304 and designed a shroud for the engine, which prompted the nickname of the "Bullet". However, one engine was not sufficient to protect the service and the streamlined blue-and-gray train could often be found trailing a non-streamlined green-and-gold Pacific. When President Roy White assumed office in 1941, he ordered all the engines painted blue, and just prior to that the motive power people had given up in disgust and ordered the shroud removed from the 5304. After the war was over, the B&O decided to give streamlining another try and this time they took *four* locomotives, 5301 through 5304, and streamlined them for the *Cincinnatian,* a Baltimore-Cincinnati express. However, this time the B&O did not retain an outside designer, but turned the work over to its first woman civil engineer, Olive Dennis. Dennis is another shining personality in the long list of famous American railroaders. She initially took her degree in mathematics and taught it for a number of years, but returned to Cornell Univeristy and became in 1920 Cornell's second women engineering graduate. Armed with a civil engineering degree, she took a position in the bridge department of the B&O as a draftsman. But "Uncle Dan" Willard took a personal interest in her and made her responsible for the quality of passenger service. For twenty-four years she held this position as Engineer of Service, riding the B&O's trains and working with both the mechanical department and the passenger traffic department to improve the quality of B&O service. Her first job was to conduct the surveys for the connecting New York bus service of the B&O. Then turning to her aesthetic talents, she designed the B&O's centennary dining-car china, which remain to this day one of the most famous china designs of all time. She worked to design new reclining coach seats and coordinated the interiors of the 1939 *Royal Blue.* A woman of amazingly diverse talents, she studied at the Baltimore Conservatory of Music and headed up the B&O Women's Music Club, back in an age when the railroads were not only an economic, but a social and cultural force in the community as well. During the Second World War, she worked for the government in aiding the transition of women into wartime railroad jobs. In 1946, she turned her talents to locomotives in designing the streamlining for the new *Cincinnatian* engines. Reportedly, she designed the shroud with nothing more sophisticated than a simple drafting triangle. The new design preserved much of the original Kuhler feeling, and yet was distinctive in its own right.

BELOW: Olive Dennis' 5304 on display at the Chicago Railroad Fair in 1948.

JOHN KRAUSE

JOHN KRAUSE

ABOVE: The 1052, an L-1a class 0-8-0 switcher, shunts passenger cars in the yard at Cumberland. The class dates to 1926 when they were outfitted as 0-8-0's by rebuilding older class E-24 2-8-0's. The E-24's in turn had been produced by a number of plants of the American Locomotive Company between 1902 and 1904. The most prominent feature of these engines is the Belpaire firebox with its unusual squared-off appearance, a result of trying to design a firebox in which all of the supporting stays would meet the sheets at right angles. This supposedly produced a stronger and more durable firebox and the Belpaire type was standard on all Pennsylvania Railroad locomotives. It's a bit difficult to believe that a grimy switcher shuffling cars in the mountains of Maryland could have a relation to the machinations of two financial giants, but such is the case. In 1896, as a result of the Panic of 1893, the B&O found itself in receivership. They had borrowed huge sums for expansion and the depressed business state made repayment impossible, so they turned to the courts for relief. They were out of receivership again by the turn of the century, but part of the reorganization plan had involved substantial new issues of stock, which found their way into the hands of the Pennsylvania in 1901. The arch-rival from Philadelphia now had the Baltimore road under its control and they promptly installed Leonor F. Loree as the new president. It was during Loree's term that the E-24's were purchased and they were built directly from the plans of the Pennsylvania's H-6 class Consolidation types. A brilliant engineer and an 18-year Pennsylvania veteran, Loree left shortly afterwards for a long career with the Delaware and Hudson, but his legacy of Pennsy engines remained on the B&O for almost fifty years afterwards. But there was more to the story than simply the mighty Pennsylvania swallowing up a competitor, for the PRR had spent a vast fortune buying control of the Chesapeake & Ohio and the Norfolk & Western, also large coal roads. The man behind all of this was Alexander J. Cassett, the president and chief architect of "The Standard Railroad of the World". He had declared a truce with his arch-rival, the Vanderbilts of the New York Central, and together they had set out to gain control of all the Appalachin coal roads. Their purpose was to end the practice of rebates, a device whereby large shippers, most notably the steel companies, could demand that the railroads kick back part of the freight rate under the table or threaten to take their

JOHN KRAUSE

business elsewhere. With all of the coal roads under their thumb, Cassett and Vanderbilt simply announced that there would be no more rebates and the insidious business of playing off one road against the other came to a sudden halt. In all likelihood the Pennsylvania would have kept its B&O stock indefinitely. But a new President, Theodore Roosevelt, had goaded the Supreme Court into dusting off the Sherman Anti-Trust Act and using it against what he considered unholy alliances. The Pennsy could see what was coming: in 1906 they sold half of their holdings to the Union Pacific, a railroad belonging to Edward H. Harriman, who was also influential on the B&O board. Then Harriman got himself in trouble in 1913 when the Supreme Court ordered him to dispose of his Southern Pacific holdings. He accomplished this by trading the SP stock off to the Pennsylvania in return for the remaining B&O stock that they held. In the final move, Union Pacific distributed all of its B&O stock to its shareholders as a *pro-rata* dividend and thus finally ended any domination of the B&O by outside roads. ABOVE: Our other eight-wheel switcher, the 684, is also a legacy of the Pennsylvania domination of the B&O, but in a somewhat different fashion. In 1903, Leonor F. Loree brought in another Pennsylvania man to head the motive power department: John E. Muhlfeld. Muhlfeld occupies a bright spot in the list of American motive-power men for designing the very first articulated Mallet locomotive in the U.S. But in 1905 and 1906, he went shopping for more 2-8-0's and had the E-27 class built at the Schenectady plant of American Locomotive. For some reason, Muhlfeld disdained the Belpaire firebox and designed the engines with a conventional firebox. But just like the earlier E-24's, the E-27's also began to disappear inside the shops between 1926 and 1929 to emerge again as 0-8-0 switchers. The 684 seen here was converted from the former 2631 in 1928. And to add a final touch to the whole story, John E. Muhlfeld left the B&O in 1908 to join his old boss on the Delaware & Hudson. Loree and Muhlfeld made more locomotive history on the D&H with their experimental engines, which included ultra-high pressure compounds and America's first all-welded boiler. In the field of esoteric locomotives, Muhlfeld was probably the only man to equal the B&O's own Col. Emerson.

LEFT: A Mikado heads a local freight out of Cumberland bound for Connellsville, Pa. The line to Pittsburgh heads out of Cumberland up through the "Narrows", the popular name for the valley of Evitt's Creek. The mountains rise up on both sides of the creek and squeeze in both the B&O on one bank and the Western Maryland on the other side. The Western Maryland parallels the B&O to Connellsville where it connects with other roads to Pittsburgh and the west. Like the B&O, it was conceived in Baltimore and received the city's financial aid in building it. Both railroads are part of today's Chessie System. The 4709 heading up the local came to the B&O in 1932 when they absorbed the Buffalo, Rochester & Pittsburgh. We will be taking a closer look not only at the engines, but at the BR&P itself later on, so for now a good look at the B&O's own Mikados is in order. RIGHT: The 4578 was a Q-3 class, one of a hundred engines (4500-4599) delivered to the B&O in 1918. The 2-8-2 type had first been designed by the Baldwin Locomotive Works and not for an American railroad, but rather for the Japanese government line. This is where the 2-8-2 acquired the name of the "Mikado" type, a reference to the popular Gilbert and Sullivan comic opera of the same name. It proved to be such an improvement over the 2-8-0, with its larger firebox supported on the trailer wheels, that large numbers of them were built in the ten years before World War I. Then came the war and a number of developments that would effect locomotive design for many years after the conflict had ended. Much of what transpired involved the B&O prominently. When war was declared in April of 1917, President Wilson immediately contacted the heads of all the major railroads and asked them to organize an industry board to coordinate the activities of all the lines in the country. The new board elected as their chairman none other than the B&O's own Daniel Willard. They worked together quite well, putting aside traditional rivalries in the name of national defense, until

JOHN KRAUSE

the final days of 1917, Wilson bowed to the politicians and signed an order giving the government complete control. He created the United States Railroad Administration, a cumbersome bureaucracy that wreaked havoc upon the railroads. It was headed by the Secretary of the Treasury, William G. McAdoo, who not coincidentally was Wilson's son-in-law. The only positive benefit of the U.S.R.A. control was the formation of a committee made up of representatives of the major locomotive and car builders, who formulated standard designs for locomotives and cars. These standards were still being followed well into the late 1920's and introduced a measure of standardization and economy into the railroad system that no one had been able to accomplish previously. The very first U.S.R.A. locomotives to be built were the hundred light Mikados for the B&O. Of all the U.S.R.A. designs, the light Mikado would find its way onto more roads than any other design. The U.S.R.A. Mikes were such a success that the B&O purchased another 135 Q-4 class 2-8-2's in the next five years. The similarities between the two classes are apparent, but the Q-4's were much heavier machines, weighing almost twice as much as the "war babies". The most prominent difference of course, is the Vanderbuilt tender on the later engines. The Vanderbuilt's cylindrical design used much less steel than a square tender and possessed as much strength without the necessity of a heavy underframe. Both engines also possess a distinctly B&O feature: note the awkward-looking extension of the rear of the cab. Later locomotives with their larger boilers left little room in the cab for the head brakeman's traditional seat on the left side of the cab. Many roads solved this problem by erecting a small shelter or "doghouse" on the back of the tender. The B&O instead lengthened the left side only of the cabs on some engines to provide a seat for the head man, giving the cab a sort of curious, asymmetrical look. In this case both the 4578 and the 4632 have received the treatment.

ROBERT F. COLLINS

PHILLIP A. RONFOR

ROBERT F. COLLINS

LEFT: The westbound *Washingtonian,* Train 21, heads up the Narrows out of Cumberland behind the 5579. Although the B&O had rails to Cleveland by the way of a branch from Akron, Train 21 went only as far as Pittsburgh on the B&O. The train then had rights over the Pittsburgh & Lake Erie to Youngstown and over the Erie through to Cleveland. Notice that the express car on the head end is another of those rebuilt troop sleepers. In fact, the locomotive itself is another product of World War II; the 5579 is one of the T-3 class Mountains built by the B&O beginning in 1942. But we have to go back much earlier to find the first 4-8-2 on the B&O, back to 1925 when Col. Emerson took the boiler of an S-class 2-10-2 and mounted it on a new 4-8-2 chassis. He made another one the next year, but apparently his attentions were then occupied elsewhere and the B&O got along with heavy Pacifics instead of Mountains. The Colonel took another stab in 1930 with a pair of Mountains equipped for a test, one with a plain firebox and one with a water-tube box. Emerson retired less than a month after Pearl Harbor and, as mentioned, the wartime production of diesel locomotives was severely restricted. But the B&O needed something bigger than Pacifics to cope with the wartime traffic, and the new man at Baltimore, A.K. Galloway, opted for the 4-8-2 type. As an economy measure, he recycled the boiler shells of old Pacifics and Mikados, adding an extra section, or boiler course to increase the steaming capacity. Mounted on a new cast steel bed, the old lengthened boiler looked somewhat incongruous and the engines weren't exactly an aesthetic delight. But they worked so

well that the Mt. Clare Shops continued to crank them out right up until 1948. TOP: A portrait of the 5580, both engines were built in the final year of the war. But notice that one has a Vanderbilt tender, the other a square tender; the tender on the 5579 was added in the early 1950's when the B&O decided to try out some giant 65-foot Vanderbilt tenders on a handful of the T-3's. They worked well, but the spreading dieselization made the building of any more an exercise in futility. BOTTOM: Something of a stranger: the 5652, a T-4 class Mountain. The end of World War II produced an interesting situation in the U.S. with locomotives. With the restrictions lifted on diesel production, many roads went on a buying spree which saw four- and five-year old modern steamers shoved off on sidetracks in favor of the diesel. This put a terrific number of modern steamers on the secondhand market at bargain prices. The B&O needed new power badly, but as a coal road they were still committed to the steam engine for road power. Although Mt. Clare was turning out T-3's, the B&O took advantage of the situation and picked up thirteen heavy Mountains secondhand from the Boston & Maine. Built by Baldwin between 1935 and 1940, the lucky thirteen (5550-5562) were heavier and more powerful than the T-3's by a substantial margin and proved to be a wise purchase. And in a curious twist of fate, the 1944 group of 4-8-2's which the Boston & Maine hung onto ended up in the boneyard in the early 1950's, while their older sisters ran in Ohio and Indiana on the B&O until 1958.

ROBERT F. COLLINS

ROBERT F. COLLINS

JOHN KRAUSE

JOHN KRAUSE

LEFT: A "Big Six" heads west out of Cumberland, the bridge in the distance brings the Western Maryland across the B&O and down into town. The 6000-series 2-10-2's were indeed big, and although articulated Mallets ruled all of the B&O's other helper grades, the grade west of Cumberland from Hyndman to Sand Patch tunnel was exclusively the province of the "Big Sixes". The B&O had got their first 2-10-2's in 1914, when the Santa Fe type, as they were called, was being hailed as the ultimate in a rigid-wheelbase freight engine. The thirty-one engines (6000-6030) from Baldwin lived up to their promise and during the great postwar locomotive buildup, the B&O went back and purchased a grand total of 125 Santa Fe's (6100-6224). The postwar engines had larger drivers and could move a little faster, and had much larger tenders, but otherwise the differences were minimal. One unique feature of the later S-1 class was the fact that 50 of the engines had been turned out by the Lima Locomotive Works of Lima, Ohio. In its early years, the B&O had been quite democratic, buying their power from both Baldwin of Philadelphia and from the host of plants that made up the American Locomotive Company (Alco), the Lima Works not appearing on the scene until well into the twentieth century. Remembering that it was Sam Vauclain of Baldwin who got Col. Emerson his job on the B&O, it is not surprising that the B&O patronized the Philadelphia builder almost exclusively after Emerson's arrival, despite the fact that Lima was an on-line B&O city also. But apparently when the S-1's were being ordered, the era of "Coolidge prosperity" had produced such a backlog of locomotive orders that the Colonel was forced to give part of the business to Lima. They would prove to be the only Lima power on the B&O and the name of Alco would not be seen until 1943, not on a steam locomotive but adorning the flanks of a diesel. The two locomotives seen represent both builders and both of the S-1 orders. The 6197 is a 1926 product of Lima. ABOVE: The 6135 was part of the 1923-24 order from Baldwin.

JOHN KRAUSE

LEFT: An FT combination pulls down into Cumberland with a long solid string of refrigerator cars from the west. The FT model was a landmark in American railroading, the first mass-production diesel freight locomotive. Introduced by the Electro-Motive Division of General Motors in 1939, the first four-unit demonstrator engines toured the U.S. on 103 different railroads. The impressive records that they set doomed the steam locomotive to extinction and proved convincingly that the diesel was not just a glamourous showpiece for passenger service, but a rugged workhorse that could handle heavy freight. Despite the wartime restrictions on diesel production that we've mentioned, the B&O did manage to get their first six FT-sets in 1942. We say "sets" for a particular reason: on a steam locomotive the engine and tender were more-or-less permanently joined with a solid drawbar rather than couplers, and the FT carried over this tradition with a drawbar between the A and B units. As on many other roads, the B&O always considered the A-B pair to be a single locomotive. When the units were purchased, they were numbered 101, 103, and 105 for three of the A-B sets, and 101A, 103A, and 105A for the other three sets. The rationale was apparently based on the fact that four units was the customary lash-up, but "we might change our mind later so let's leave a hole just in case". They changed their mind: not too many years after the war, the "A" suffix was dropped and 101A became simply 102, 103A became 104, and so forth. In 1943, the B&O talked the government out of six more FT's, nos. 107, 107A to 111, 111A. Like the first group, these eventually became simply 107 through 112. The 108 is one of this group. Remember that through all this numbers game, the poor old B unit just tagged along with no identification of its own.

TOP RIGHT: The 59 is the passenger counterpart of the FT: the E-6, EMD's first real production model passenger diesel. We've discussed the E-6 before, but we should note that it was not the first passenger diesel on the B&O. The fledgling Electro-Motive Corporation had been born in the midst of the Depression and set out to produce diesel locomotives. Their first triumphs were really power cars that were an integral part of a complete train; it was the famous no. 50 that they built for the B&O in 1935 that was the first true self-contained locomotive. An ugly-looking boxcab unit, the 50 left the B&O and went to the Alton Railroad when the B&O cut the Alton loose on its own in 1942. In 1937, the Electro-Motive Corporation had become a part of General Motors and they turned out six EA sets for the B&O. These were another first: the first streamlined diesel units in the U.S. and they owed their design to no less a figure than Henry Dreyfus, who had scored another design triumph for GM with his famous port-holed Buick automobile. The E-1 through E-5 models further refined the basic design until EMD finally settled down with the E-6 as a stock-model passenger locomotive. BOTTOM RIGHT: Even the impressive 4000 horsepower output of the 61 needs some help on the climb up to Sand Patch tunnel; in this case a P-ld Pacific. We should probably say the 61 and 61X; the B units on the passenger engines were tied to the A's with couplers and were quite easily separated, so they were given their own number. The partner to 61 would just be 61X; like the freight units, this was changed in the general 1956 renumbering and the B units got their own individual numbers. One can imagine the old-time steam men at Baltimore flooding the inter-office mail with memos as they tried to decide how to number and classify the new beast. The 5048 is one of those P-lc engines built in the late 20's from old Mikados and subsequently rebuilt as P-ld's with larger tenders and modern appliances in the early 1940's. The diesel-steam combination is heading up westbound Train 9, the *Washington-Pittsburgh-Chicago Express;* not a very romantic name as trains go, but there was no mistaking where it would take you.

JOHN KRAUSE

ROBERT F. COLLINS

JOHN KEAUSE

ABOVE: The 5083 running light back to Cumberland in the summer of 1948; having assisted a train up to Sand Patch tunnel, she's on her way back to Cumberland to await the next call for an assist. At this time, the 5083 was amongst the oldest Pacifics on the B&O. The very first 4-6-2's had come from the Schenectady plant of American Locomotive in 1906 and were an instant success, going through a number of rebuildings and finally disappearing from the roster in the late 1940's. The next batch came from Baldwin in 1911, the P-1's (5050-5059) and the just slightly heavier P-1a's (5060-5089). These engines endured a lot of rebuilding: The cylinders were enlarged, then some had the stroke shortened, a few were given Baker valve gear; then in the 1929-1940 period, they received the large tenders and extensive upgrading that made them P-1d's and enabled them to survive through to the final days of steam. RIGHT: Five years later, almost to the day, 5083 showed up at Hyndman, Pa. and was caught looking just as good as she did in 1948. The 5083 and diesel 60 are walking right through Hyndman with a westbound passenger train and heading right into the Sand Patch grade. The "Big Six" at the right is stopped to pick up two more of its brethen as pushers before tackling the grade. At Hyndman, 14 miles above Cumberland and now into Pennsylvania, the B&O rails turn from their northerly course and head due west up the 19-mile Sand Patch grade. Passenger trains would get their helper at Cumberland to avoid any delay, but the freights would stop at Hyndman and pick up the pushers.

ROBERT F. COLLINS

ROBERT F. COLLINS

The spectacle of three "Big Sixes" working through their preserve on the way up to Sand Patch is a railroad fan's reward. The Mallets were excluded from the Sand Patch grade and helper work was the exclusive province of the 2-10-2's until the diesels arrived. ABOVE: The 6119 leads the way at Hyndman. OPPOSITE: The 6135 and 6145 shove hard against the substantial bulk of a "wagon-top" caboose. We've discussed the contributions of the B&O's Col. Emerson to locomotive development in the U.S., but it's often forgotten that the B&O was in the forefront of car design too. Like Emerson in the locomotive department, the guiding light of the car department was John J. Tatum. He had first hired out to the B&O on his *thirteenth* birthday in 1879 as a messenger boy and subsequently became an apprentice at the old Mt. Clare shops in Baltimore. Rising through the ranks, he eventually became General Superintendent of the car department in 1925 and in the course of his tenure in the office, he amassed a total of 66 patents and 8 copyrights for improved designs of cars and car parts. The "wagon-tops" were first introduced at a public display in the Washington Union Station in the spring of 1935. Not merely one car, but eight separate designs of box and covered hopper cars. Tatum literally tried everything: special steel and aluminum alloys, corrugated side sheets, boxcars with roof hatches and hopper outlets for bulk loadings, all built to the wagon-top configuration. The rationale of the design was that the continous rib—running up one side, across the roof, and back down the other side—would give more strength and rigidity to the cars. It was a well-established fact that after many years of improvements, the roof still remained the weakest part of a box car and the wagon-top aimed at curing this problem. The following year, 1936, Tatum began a program of building cabooses to the wagon-top design and they rolled out of Mt. Clare, Cumberland, and Keyser shops right through to 1945. Even today, the wagon-top hacks still populate the Chessie System in great numbers, while their boxcar brethren roam the country in interchange service. Like the Big Sixes, the mention of the wagon-tops calls nothing else to mind but B&O.

ROBERT F. COLLINS

ROBERT F. COLLINS

LEFT: One of the giant EM-1's lifting 87 cars up Sand Patch grade in the twilight year of 1955. Near the town of Manila, Pa., the 7606 has only a few miles to go before reaching the summit at Sand Patch tunnel and only a few months to go before being shoved west into West Virginia and Ohio for her final few years of service handling lake coal trains. TOP RIGHT: A pair of "Big Sixes"—the 6113 and the 6197—are shoving hard on the rear end. Notice that the upgrade track is almost white with the countless tons of sand that have been spread on the rails for traction by ascending trains. BOTTOM RIGHT: A look at the long and massive lines of the EM-1's. The 2-8-8-4's were built by Baldwin during the Second World War, the 7600-7619 in 1944 and the 7620-7629 in 1945, thirty giants in all. The 2-8-8-4, occasionally referred to as the "Yellowstone" type, was first introduced by the American Locomotive Company in 1928 when they built a single locomotive for the Northern Pacific. Although Alco built the very first Yellowstone, named after the national park traversed by the NP, they never built another one. They were underbid by Baldwin for the remainder of the NP's 2-8-8-4's. The Lima Locomotive Works got in the act with a group of 2-8-8-4's for the Southern Pacific and then Baldwin built some more for the ore-hauling Duluth Missabe and Iron Range. The construction of the B&O's EM-1's closed the book on the Yellowstone type. Reportedly, the B&O wanted diesels but the government wouldn't let them have them and they settled instead for the EM-1's. But despite the wartime rationing of diesel power, it's doubtful if anyone complained too much when they saw what they had instead.

ROBERT F. COLLINS

ROBERT F. COLLINS

ROBERT F. COLLINS

ABOVE: The 7626, the last of the class, is making much better time up through Manila with a train of 77 empties, requiring the services of only one of the 2-10-2's. The brute size of the EM-1's is verified by the statistics: in working order, they weighed 505 tons, the largest piece of machinery that even the well-built line of the B&O mains could support. The two equal-sized cylinders on the front and rear engines testify that the engines are simple articulateds; by the time the EM-1's were built, the idea of compounding or using the steam twice had long been discarded. They boasted every modern appliance that was available and were the pinnacle of locomotive development on the B&O. **RIGHT**: One of the ubiquitous P-ld Pacifics, the 5083, bursts forth from the west portal of Sand Patch tunnel heading a double-headed westbound *Washingtonian*. The tunnel, nearly a mile in length, pierces the Alleghenies at one of their highest points. The original bore dated to the Civil War and was a single-track, timber-lined monstrosity that was replaced in the years just before World War I as part of President Daniel Willard's determined plan to see all of the main line double-tracked. To get the maximum usefulness out of the tunnel, it was signalled for movement in either direction on both tracks and was protected at each end by a tower controlling the movements. The end of the steam era put an end to the daily spectacles that once were commonplace on the Sand Patch grade. But that did not mean that history could not repeat itself, for 1977 was the B&O's 150th anniversary and the anniversary was fittingly commemorated by the running of the *Chessie Steam Special*. Headed by a Reading 4-8-4, the 2101, the *Steam Special* roamed the Chessie System, bringing back fond memories of the steam era introducing thousands of younger people to the fascination of steam railroading. The high point of the year came early in the season as the 2101 assaulted Sand Patch with 18 loaded passenger cars. Down on her knees at 4 mph, the 4-8-4 held on and triumphantly topped over the grade and burst through the tunnel in a truly memorable moment.

WILLIAM P. PRICE

ROBERT F. COLLINS

ROBERT F. COLLINS

LEFT: A pair of ex-Buffalo, Rochester & Pittsburgh 2-8-2's at Keystone, Pa. The former BR&P Mikes are approaching Sand Patch tunnel from the west side with a 33-car local freight. The realistically named Buffalo, Rochester & Pittsburgh—it went exactly where it's corporate title said it did—had an excellent fleet of locomotives that passed to the B&O when operation of the BR&P was assumed in 1932. ABOVE: A portrait of the 4708, one of the first group of Mikados purchased from Alco in 1912. The BR&P bought many of their locomotives in small lots over a period of years. The first 2-8-2's came from the Brooks Works of Alco at Dunkirk, N.Y. in 1912 and then they went back again in 1913 and 1917 until they had a total of 48 engines, all essentially identical. The class Q-10 locomotives were numbered 4700-4747 on the B&O. They were quite similar to a number of other Alco Mikados built for various roads in the ten years prior to the first World War. Apparently because the Brooks Works was the nearest builder to the BR&P, they purchased virtually all of their power from the Alco plant. When the B&O assumed operation, the large fleet of Alco engines joined a roster that was almost entirely Baldwin-built engines. And unlike many of the other absorbed roads in the B&O system, the BR&P engines were not confined to their old home rails but rather wandered quite extensively around the system.

ROBERT F. COLLINS

The ungainly-looking beast heading up a train of 82 loads of coal at Keystone, is one of the B&O's many compound articulated locomotives. The compound articulated was an import, developed in France by Anatole Mallet in 1885 and first imported to America by the B&O's John E Muhlfeld. Reportedly, president Leonor F. Loree had heard of successful Mallets being used in Switzerland and Russia and was sufficiently intrigued to order Muhlfeld to construct one for tests on the B&O. Muhlfeld worked with Alco to design and build the 2400, known as "Old Maude" after a comic-strip character of the day, a rather cantankerous old mule. The 2400 was a true Mallet: It was an 0-6-6-0 arranged as a compound articulated. Compounding was an idea that looked good on paper: over half of a locomotive's generated heat went up the stack with the steam exhaust; why not try to use it over a second time before exhausting it? Thus the rear engine got live steam right from the boiler and a set of flexible pipes carried the steam up to the front engine where it was "compounded" or used a second time. Of course the pressure drop made much larger cylinders necessary in order to get any useful work out of the lower pressure and the oversized front cylinders became the hallmark of the true compound. Articulated means jointed and for such a large locomotive to be able to get around curves, it was jointed at the center of the frames. The rear engine was rigidly attached to the boiler and cab in the usual fashion. But the front engine was connected to the rear by a giant swivel pin which allowed it to follow the track on curves. The front of the boiler rested its heavy weight on a sliding plate that put the weight on the front engine drivers to give traction, yet allowed the front engine to swivel freely. As we said, compounding looked good on paper, but engineers failed to consider the extra maintenance costs involved and as labor costs rose, they began to rapidly outstrip the savings in fuel. Pleased with the performance of Old Maude, the B&O tried an experiment in building their own Mallets in 1911 and then gave up and purchased thirty 0-8-8-0's from Baldwin in the years 1911 to 1913. However, the lack of a lead pair of wheels on these locomotives made it impossible to run them at more than a fast walk without the fear of the heavily-loaded drivers climbing right over and off the rails on a curve. So in 1916, a pair of pony wheels was added to guide the locos into curves and the B&O had Baldwin build 30 new 2-8-8-0's. The new design was a success and they went back for thirty more the next year. LEFT: The year is 1951 and all of the old 0-8-8-0's have been scrapped, but the 7136, a Baldwin graduate of 1917, is still going strong with its original compound arrangement. The bulk of the first three EL-classes had been rebuilt to simple engines, whereby all four cylinders got live steam. TOP RIGHT: The 7212 shown working with an ex-BR&P Mike has also escaped the treatment, although the trip to the scrapyard is not very far away. BOTTOM RIGHT: The last of the new 2-8-8-0's: the 7155 is part of a group of 26 U.S.R.A. designs (7145-7170) delivered in 1919 and 1920. Notice the equal-sized cylinders, a tip-off that the engine is a simple articulated. Although built as compounds, all but two of the class had been simpled by 1930.

ROBERT F. COLLINS

ROBERT F. COLLINS

ROBERT F. COLLINS

To zero in on a train gives us both the detail of the locomotives and a feeling for the sheer size and impressiveness of them. But occasionally it's a good idea to step back, for impressive as the train itself can be, the scenery and sheer breadth of the terrain can often be equally or even more impressive. Sometimes in our fascination with the locomotives and cars and some of the physical plant of the railroad, we often forget that the essence of the railroad is a transportation system that can move vast tonnages over equally vast distances. Here we see an overview of the train seen at Keystone on the previous pages further down the hill at Meyersdale, Pa. Given an average of 50 to 55 tons of coal in each car, the figures mount up quickly into a very heavy train and explain the presence of so much power on both ends of the long drag. It's still somewhat mind-boggling today to think that the men of Baltimore in 1827 could actually propose to build a railroad for 400 miles through the heart of the Alleghenies to the Ohio River, and even more incredible to realize that they accomplished it. Undoubtedly they set a pace for others to follow; if Baltimore could be tied to the Ohio valley, then why could not one end of the country be tied to the other by iron rails? It was and other transcontinentals followed, while a fabric of smaller lines weaved their way across the land and drew the vast land together into a unified country.

ROBERT F. COLLINS

ROBERT F. COLLINS

ROBERT F. COLLINS

We've mentioned the old Buffalo, Rochester and Pittsburgh Railway a number of times and now it's time to take a look at some of it. These two scenes are both on the Indiana branch, which is not in the Midwest, but rather in Indiana County, Pennsylvania, in the heart of the Pittsburgh-Johnstown area of coal mines and steel mills. The 36-mile branch to Indiana comes off the main at Punxsutawney, the town famous for its groundhog, "Punxsutawney Phil", whose weather predictions are broadcast worldwide each February second. ABOVE: Although the line runs roughly southeast, it is westbound on the timetable and the 7166 is heading west with 33 empty hoppers. The engine is one of the U.S.R.A. 2-8-8-0's that has been rebuilt simple and is bound for the mines in the Indiana area. The World War I veteran is near Rossiter in December of 1954 and is running out its last miles. RIGHT: A somewhat older EL-3a Mallet, the 7121, with 65 cars at Locust is about 9 miles west of Punxsutawney. The isolation of the area is evident, and when this photo was taken in the late 1940's the branch was still served four times a day by a gas-electric car that provided rudimentary passenger service as far as Indiana. Near Indiana a number of coal branches fanned out from the line to tap the maze of coal mines in the area. The line then continued for another 30 miles from Indiana to Vintondale and a connection with both the Pennsylvania Railroad and the shortline Cambria & Indiana. The C&I was controlled by Bethlehem Steel and was used principally to bring coal to the giant Bethlehem complex at Johnstown.

7121

JOHN KRAUSE

LEFT: A westbound passenger train leaves Mt. Jewett, Pa. in 1951 bound for Pittsburgh. Like the Mikado types, the BR&P picked up its Pacific types in small lots over a number of years and like the Mikes, the 4-6-2's were all from Brooks. The numbers ran from 5140 to 5148 and 5185 to 5192, a total of seventeen engines in all from 1912 to 1918 and all virtually identical. They served the B&O until the mid-fifties when the diesels finally caught up with them. In the late 1940's and early 1950's, the B&O had six passenger trains a day running on the old BR&P. Separate sections for Buffalo and Rochester would be combined or split at East Salamanca, N.Y., although the track actually split about 13 miles further up the line. Originally the predecessors of the BR&P operated only in New York until an 1887 merger put the Buffalo, Rochester & Pittsburgh Railway together in both New York and Pennsylvania. At first Punxsutawney was the end of the line, but turn-of-the century expansion took the BR&P first to Butler and then to New Castle. Rights were secured to run over the B&O itself from Butler into Pittsburgh and the extension to New Castle brought BR&P rails to within 10 miles of the Ohio border. A branch from Rochester to Genesee Docks on Lake Ontario gave the BR&P car-ferry access to the Grand Trunk lines in Canada. All in all, it was a very impressive, well-run, and successful railroad. TOP RIGHT One of the ex-BR&P 2-6-6-2 Mallets pulls by the Mt. Jewett station in the fall of 1948 heading west. We're going to take a closer look at these engines in just a moment. The BR&P was full of backwards timetable directions; although it essentially ran almost due north and south, it was operated under the traditional east-west system of timetables, Pittsburgh being the west end and Buffalo and Rochester being the east end of the road. In the spring of 1952, we're west of the station and nearly all of the old Mallets have made the last trip to the scrapyard. BOTTOM RIGHT: A three-unit F3 combination heads west out of Mt. Jewett. The diesel came from the Electro-Motive Division of General Motors in 1948 and 1949; being the tail end of F3 production, they look externally just like their successors, the improved F7 model introduced in 1949. Reflecting the motive-power department's apparent schizophrenia over diesel numbers, they were delivered in three-unit A-B-A combinations, numbered 153, 153X, 153A through 171, 171X, 171A; odd numbers only. For those who are still snowed under by the so-called "new math", that makes 20 combos or 60 individual locomotives. To everyone's great relief, the "A" and "X" suffixes were discarded in 1956 and every locomotive was given its own number.

ROBERT F. COLLINS

JOHN KRAUSE

ROBERT F. COLLINS

LEFT: The 7533 is nearing the top of hill between Bradford and Mt. Jewett going west with a long drag of 105 cars in the early fall of 1949. The BR&P Mallets can hardly be called good-looking locomotives, but they are interesting. Pursuing their policy of power in dribs and drabs, the BR&P picked up their first five 2-6-6-2's in 1914 from Alco, of course. Then in 1917 and 1918 they went on a spree and bought 36 engines; one more purchase in 1923 brought the total up to fifty-five engines, nos. 7500 to 7554. Following the policy of the day, they were all compound articulated; but in later years, their differences stood out in contrast to the B&O's own Mallets. The B&O disdained the trailer wheels on their engines, but the BR&P used them for the extra support not only on the 2-6-6-2's, but on two larger classes of 2-8-8-2's they also owned. And most of the B&O's compounds were simpled by 1930, while the BR&P engines retained their outsized front cylinders right to the end, with the compound engine being actuated by the even more outdated Stephenson valve gear. The high temperature of superheated steam, introduced in the years after 1900, had been too much for the old Stephenson gear and it fell into disuse in favor of newer gears and piston valves. But the low pressure and temperature found in the front-end engine of a compound could be easily handled by the Stephenson gear and the old-style "D" valves (so-called because the valve looked like a capital "D" laid on its back). TOP RIGHT: another 2-6-6-2, the 7521, shoves on the rear against a heavily-built caboose that also came from the BR&P. The C-2659 was one of a group of 50 hacks that came from the on-line plant of the old Standard Steel Car Company at Butler in 1923. In 1930, Standard Steel was absorbed by the Pullman Company, who was seeking to enter the freight car market. In 1934, Pullman-Standard was formed and they remain today one of the foremost builders of freight and passenger equipment; the old Standard Steel plant at Butler remains one of Pullman-Standard's principal facilities. BOTTOM RIGHT: A formal portrait of the 7539; the clutter of flexible steam delivery pipes and reverse linkage underneath the running boards forced the air tanks from their usual location up to a high perch on top of the boiler.

ROBERT F. COLLINS

ROBERT F. COLLINS

JOHN KRAUSE

LEFT: South of Bradford, Pa., an ex-BR&P Pacific heads west for Pittsburgh. The number of head-end cars suggests a good business in mail and express was handled on these trains. Bradford was a division point on the BR&P until shortly after the turn of the century, when the division headquarters were removed to East Salamanca, N.Y., where the BR&P crossed the Erie mainline. The Erie operated a local service themselves from East Salamanca as far as Bradford and a freight-only branch of the Pennsylvania came down from New York also. TOP RIGHT: The 5148 which came from Brooks in 1913, continuing the design purchased the previous year. Another order in 1918 would bring the total up to 17 engines. The BR&P went back to Brooks one more time in 1923 to buy five more Pacifics, but on their last order they tried a new wrinkle. BOTTOM RIGHT: Numbers 5260 to 5264, were essentially identical to their older brethern, but the pistons had both a smaller bore (or diameter) and a longer stroke. This had the effect of lowering the tractive effort, which is the amount of pull a locomotive can put on the drawbar of a train when starting it; in this case about 3000 lbs. of pull was lost. But in return, the locomotives had the ability to run with a train at higher speeds. The reader has probably wondered how the BR&P, a successful and first-class operation, came into the B&O fold. Its operation was so good that it attracted the attention of the Van Sweringen brothers of Cleveland, two of the most unusual figures to ever come on the American railroad scene. O.P. and M.J. Van Sweringen, both bachelors, had amassed a modest fortune dealing in Cleveland real estate and had gotten into the railroad business in the course of building an interurban to serve their new surburban community of Shaker Heights in Cleveland. Then they were given an opportunity to purchase the Nickel Plate Road, a railroad that largely paralleled the prosperous New York Central. The Central had gained control of the Nickel Plate and was eager to dump it off on someone. The Van Sweringens were able to talk the Cleveland banks into fronting almost the total purchase price, then they turned around and made the Nickel Plate such a fierce competitor that the Central sorely regretted ever letting them have it. With the Nickel Plate on a firm financial base and now worth millions, the brothers set out to build a rail empire. By the latter part of the 1920's, they owned a substantial or controlling interest in the Chesapeake & Ohio, the Erie, the Chicago & Eastern Illinois, the Pere Marquette, the Wheeling & Lake Erie, and the Missouri Pacific. In 1928, they turned their eye to the BR&P and bought a 67% interest, which in turn was transferred to the Alleghany Corporation, the organization that handled all their railroad properties. It's not clear why, but shortly afterward Alleghany offered to sell the whole works to the B&O, who jumped at the offer. The sale was approved by the ICC and completed in 1930, with the remainder of the BR&P stockholders getting a guaranteed annual return. After sorting out the details, the B&O took over formal operation on Jan. 1, 1932. Included in the transfer were 241 locomotives and roughly 12,500 freight cars plus a top-notch piece of railroad. The B&O definitely got themselves a good deal.

ROBERT F. COLLINS

ROBERT F. COLLINS

ROBERT F. COLLINS

ROBERT F. COLLINS

ROBERT F. COLLINS

TOP LEFT: The 3031 is an ex-BR&P 2-8-0, one of a fleet of 65 engines purchased from Boooks. They were bought from 1902 to 1909 in small lots and for some reason were numbered in the most scattershot method possible: they skipped numbers, backed up, jumped ahead; most unusual in the BR&P's otherwise well-ordered roster. On the B&O, the locomotives ended up in the range from 3009 to 3082, still a jumble of disconnected numbers. The idea of buying locomotives in small lots over a period of time is not as strange as it may seem at first, and was practiced by a number of small-to-medium sized roads. Buying small lots meant paying cash, which in turn avoided the substantial interest charges that were incurred with borrowed money. Once the builder had the drawings and patterns made, it wasn't that difficult to crank out a few each year. Notice that the 3031 has been given a new set of Walschaerts valve gear, but still retains the original cyclinders. A device known as the Economy valve chest was designed for many of these old slide valve engines. It fit right on the old cyclinder casting and allowed the use of the more modern piston valves without the necessity of replacing the whole cylinder casting, a very large and expensive piece to replace. The Economy valve chest was just the ticket and they literally sold like hotcakes, enabling many older engines to be superheated and substantially upgraded at a nominal cost. BOTTOM LEFT: The 3141 is a 2-8-0 from the other "Buffalo" road, the Buffalo & Susquehanna, which the B&O also took over in 1932. It is quite similar to the BR&P Consolidations, and this is no surprise as they also came from Brooks in the years 1904 to 1908, with a few strays being built down at Alco's Pittsburgh plant. Numbered 3100 to 3142, these B&S engines show a few differences: the drivers are a good deal smaller and they have the canted cylinder castings with piston valves controlled by a Stephenson gear. The Stephenson gear lies entirely between the frames and its operation required an axle with a crank forged into it. As engines got heavier and axles bigger, it became more difficult to produce a cranked axle of sufficient strength. Subsequent gears like the Walschaerts did not require a crank, were more accessible for maintenance, and gave better control, for the valve motion on a locomotive could be adjusted to conditions of load and speed very much the way an automobile transmission has different gears for varying conditions. ABOVE: The 3109 is in charge of westbound Train 79, waiting to leave the station at Addison, N.Y. After World War II, only two trains, 78 and 79, provided passenger service on the old B&S, running between Addison on the Erie mainline and the remote mountain town of Galeton, Pa. Two Erie through trains, the eastbound *Atlantic Express* and the westbound *Erie Limited,* met each day at Addison in the late afternoon and the B&S accomodation was timed to meet them both. The Erie mains and the Addison station are visible behind the engine. A 75-minute layover at Addison gave the B&O crew time to turn the engine on a wye outside of town and make the Erie connections in both directions.

JOHN KRAUSE

ROBERT F. COLLINS

TOP LEFT: The 1484 running through the dense woodlands near Gaines, Pa. on the way to Addison and heading up the first of two steep mountain grades on the route. The three diminutive Atlantics—1484, 1485, and 1486—were Alco products of 1904 and 1906; the 1486 was fitted with slightly larger drivers, but otherwise differed little from the first two 4-4-2's. The 1486 suffered an early demise in the '30's, but the other two Atlantics ran until 1948. They were a railfan's delight, for the 4-4-2 was a minority wheel arrangement and there were precious few of them still running after the second World War. Just south of Gaines station, the track swung off at Gaines Junction and headed east for 9 miles to a connection with the New York Central; this had once been the original B&S mainline until the company decided to strike out for New York instead. LOWER LEFT: A freight crew pulls up to the interchange switch at Westfield, Pa., ready to drop off their cars for the New York Central; the "brains" (the conductor) has already dropped off at the switch. Westfield lay in the valley of the Cowanesque Creek and a New York Central branch came over from Lawrenceville and paralleled the B&S up the creek as far as Westfield, the site of a large tannery. Timber and coal were the reason for the existence of the B&S. The Buffalo & Susquehanna was very much a "personality" road, the work of very unique individuals; in this case the Goodyear brothers of Buffalo. Frank H. Goodyear had amassed a considerable fortune as a coal and lumber dealer in Buffalo to the point where he retired in his early '40's. But for a man of his energy, retirement was a monumental bore and he decided to go back to the source of his wealth, buying tens of thousands of acres of coal and timber lands in and around Indiana county in Pennsylvania. Coal and timber required a railroad, and Goodyear's first venture was a short line out of Austin in 1885. Then like a weed, the system grew out to reach new mines and timber cuttings, the main line from Wharton to Ansonia was opened in 1893 and the system acquired its name of the Buffalo & Susquehanna. Three years later, the B&S struck out for Wellsville, N.Y. and two years later bought an old broken-down narrow guage line to Addison, N.Y. and rebuilt it. In the years just before and after 1900, there seemed to be no end in sight to the Goodyear brothers' empire, for brother Charles W. Goodyear had joined the enterprise. The track reached south, first to Sinnemahoning and then to Sagamore, almost within reach of Pittsburgh. The B&S Coal & Coke Company was formed, steel mills were erected at Buffalo and ships of the B&S Steamship Company

JOHN KRAUSE

brought iron ore from Goodyear fields in Michigan and Minnesota. In 1906, the crowning touch was added with the extension of the mainline from Wellsville to Buffalo, bringing the B&S mileage up to almost 400 miles of mainline and branches. But being as dependent as it was on an individual, the inevitable happened: Frank Goodyear, the guiding light of the B&S, died in 1907 and the railroad quickly began to fall apart. The B&S went into receivership in 1910 and the 1913 reorganization plan called for tearing up the 7-year-old Buffalo extension; the track was torn up less than ten years after it was put down. The truncated B&S hobbled along through the 1920's until an offer was made to buy the property by the B&O. The B&O was encouraged by a 1929 consolidation plan formulated by the Interstate Commerce Commission which suggested that the B&O acquire both the B&S and the BR&P. The Federal agency was attempting to encourage the railroads to get rid of duplicate facilities; in a very rare burst of foresight, they could see that the excess and duplicating mileage would eventually drag all the roads down. The B&O operated the old B&S essentially intact through the 1930's, but a disastrous flood in July of 1942 washed out much of the track between Sinnemahoning and Burrows, all in Pennsylvania. This track included many bridges and a set of torturous switchbacks that the B&O simply couldn't justify rebuilding when the line was paralleled by so many other tracks in the same area. Much of the old B&S south of Sinnemahoning was right next to ex-BR&P trackage, so one or the other was discarded and the isolated "wishbone" of trackage left was operated independently from the rest of the B&O system. The B&O finally gave up and sold the remnants of the old B&S to the Salzberg interests in December of 1955, who organized the Wellsville, Addison & Galeton. Six of the old ex-B&S Consolidations were still stranded on the line, but continued operation of them was futile and diesel power was brought in. The B&S had always been dependent on the host of tanneries along the line; although independent from the Goodyear operations, they relied on the hemlock bark from the Goodyear sawmills as a source of tannic acid, the prime requirement for tanning hides. Thus the newly-formed WAG adopted the motto, "The Sole Leather Line". ABOVE: The 3140 pauses at the Westfield tank in 1950 for a drink of water pulled from the Cowanesque Creek just behind the tank. Despite being isolated from the rest of the system, the old B&S has apparently not been forgotten, for the tank shines with a fresh coat of paint. The photo is a slice of American pie: the peddler freight stopped for a drink at the proverbial "tank town".

RIGHT: The 5232, bursts from the portal of the tunnel at West Liberty, Pa., a small station just south of Dubois. Because of the severe grade, the engineer has to work steam through the curve and right up to the small station, and you can be sure that the mountain air is welcome relief after their short sojourn in hell. The laboring Pacific, wreathed in smoke and steam, proudly fronts the now-familiar capitol emblem; a singular moment of drama preserved for us as a part of the legacy of the 150 years of the BALTIMORE & OHIO HERITAGE!

JOHN KRAUSE